First published in the United States of America
in 2005 by Walker Publishing Company, Inc.
Distributed to the trade by Holtzbrinck
Publishers

For information about permission to reproduce
selections from this book, write to
Permissions, Walker & Company,
104 Fifth Avenue, New York, New York 10011

The artist used acrylic on illustration board to create the illustrations for this book.

Book design by Maura Fadden Rosenthal/Mspace

Visit Walker & Company's Web site at www.walkeryoungreaders.com

Printed in Hong Kong
10 9 8 7 6 5 4 3 2 1

Library of Congress Cataloging-in-Publication Data

Vieira, Linda.
    The mighty Mississippi : the life and times of America's greatest river / Linda Vieira ;
illustrations by Higgins Bond.
      p. cm.
    ISBN 0-8027-8943-9 (hardcover) -- ISBN 0-8027-8944-7 (reinforced)
  1. Mississippi River—History—Juvenile literature.   2. Mississippi
    River—Geography—Juvenile literature.   I. Bond, Higgins, ill. II. Title.

    F351.V54 2005
917.7—dc22

                                                                    2004065115

ISBN-13 978-0-8027-8943-3 (hardcover)
ISBN-13 978-0-8027-8944-0 (reinforced)

At Lake Itasca in northwestern Minnesota near the Canadian border, the mighty Mississippi River begins its long, twisting journey 2,350 miles through the heartland of the United States to the Gulf of Mexico.

Many thousands of years ago, mammoth glaciers inched southward across North America. As they began to melt, the newly freed water created huge lakes. The lakes emptied into a gigantic River Warren, which gouged out a wide swath of land now called the Mississippi River valley. Over time, the huge flow of water retreated to the banks of the Mississippi River.

Thousands of years before Europeans came to the New World, Native Americans used birchbark and dugout canoes to explore the northern and central areas of the continent along the Mississippi River.

14,000 BCE

500 CE

DRAINAGE BASIN OF THE MISSISSIPPI

The enormous watershed of the Mississippi River drains thirty-one states and two Canadian provinces and is one of the world's largest drainage basins.

Between the western Rocky Mountains and the eastern Appalachians, almost half of the United States slants inward toward the center of the continent, its water funneling into the Mississippi. Hundreds of tributaries form a network of rivers linking a third of North America by water. The Ojibwa Indians near the river's source called it Mes-sipi, "Father of Running Waters."

By about 500 CE, the Hopewell and Adena peoples of the Ohio River valley had developed a trade system along this waterway that spread from the Great Lakes to the Gulf of Mexico, from the Rockies to the Atlantic Ocean.

14,000 BCE   500 CE   1200 CE

The basin of the Upper Mississippi is a huge floodplain. The river travels 700 miles from its source before meeting the Missouri, its largest western tributary. Where they join near St. Louis, Missouri, the "Big Muddy" of the Missouri River streams separately for miles within the clear waters of the Mississippi.

The Mississippian culture of Native Americans controlled central North America for hundreds of years. Large villages linked nomadic tribes from coast to coast.

This spectacular civilization built thousands of gigantic earthen hills, or mounds, along the Mississippi and its tributaries. The urban center of Cahokia flourished until about 1200 CE as the largest community in North America, supporting almost twenty thousand people. Declining resources caused the disappearance of these ancient Mound Builders centuries before Europeans ever arrived.

14,000 BCE   500 CE   1200 CE   1682 CE

LA SALLE'S ROUTE
1679-80, 1682 ——

DE SOTO'S ROUTE — — —
CREW'S ROUTE AFTER DE SOTO'S DEATH ——

Cold northern air meets warm southern winds over the Mississippi River valley. Drenching spring rains join melting winter snows to soak the land. Swollen tributaries dump water heavy with silt into the main channel, and the river overflows.

Braving dangerous waterways, adventurous Europeans searched the unknown continent for fabled cities of gold. Spanish explorers discovered the river when Hernando de Soto journeyed northwest from Spanish Cuba looking for riches. René-Robert Cavelier Sieur de La Salle traveled south from French Canada, reaching the river's mouth at the Gulf of Mexico. He claimed the entire Mississippi River valley for France in 1682, calling it "Louisiana" to honor King Louis XIV.

14,000 BCE   500 CE   1200 CE   1682 CE   1780 CE

The Mississippi snakes along its floodplain, sculpting a twisted riverbed of hairpin turns. Floods carve new paths across the narrow loops, leaving comma-shaped oxbow lakes cut off from the main channel. Riverfront areas are often left high and dry.

During the Revolutionary War, American forces battled up and down the Mississippi and its largest eastern tributary, the Ohio. Control of river traffic in the heartland helped make the new nation victorious. After British and Indian forces were defeated in St. Louis and Cahokia, Britain gave all land east of the Mississippi River to the United States in 1783, and peace settled over the land.

The river's flowing current pulverizes its banks, dragging rocks and rubble across its bottom, depositing grains of sand into its main stream. It adds tons of sediment to debris already washed downriver from faraway mountain streams.

Pioneers on horseback and rafts and in canoes and covered wagons braved uncertain conditions to travel west across the Mississippi. Many communities and settlements were established along its banks.

In 1811, cataclysmic earthquakes in Missouri made buckling land shudder and ripple, ringing church bells in faraway cities. More than two thousand seismic waves churned the area for months, and hundreds of people were killed. Farms were swallowed by the earth, forests disappeared, whole towns were buried in quicksand, and part of the Mississippi River ran backward for hours.

Moderate climate, generous rainfall, and rich soil in the river's enormous floodplain provide near-perfect conditions for large-scale agriculture. Corn and beans developed by Native Americans in the Mississippi River valley were soon followed by farms and plantations growing rice, cotton, and tobacco. Agriculture became the economic mainstay of the heartland.

The U.S. Army sent soldiers to protect settlers from Indians, and many people were massacred. Beginning in 1838, Congress forced Native Americans living east of the Mississippi to relocate to reservations in the west. Almost a hundred thousand men, women, and children were forced to walk away from the lands of their forefathers. Thousands died along this "Trail of Tears."

14,000 BCE   500 CE   1200 CE   1682 CE   1780 CE   1811 CE   1825 CE

Drastic weather causes the river to ebb and flow. Freezing snows and driving rains change water depths and add underwater dangers. If the river freezes in winter, navigation stops.

The greatest mass exodus in the history of religious freedom in America began one freezing February night in 1846. Twelve thousand Mormons fled Nauvoo, Illinois, to avoid persecution for their beliefs.

They crossed the Mississippi on rafts amid chunks of floating ice. Some crossed over the frozen river on foot in total darkness, the first of more than seventy thousand Mormons who trekked across the wilderness in search of a safe haven.

In times of drought, the uneven riverbed of the Mississippi becomes too shallow to navigate, while torrential thunderstorms create treacherous flooding and rapids.

Hundreds of runaway slaves waded north through dangerous waters of the Mississippi and Missouri rivers. In the dark of night, they escaped to freedom through Illinois and Indiana.

States joining the Union struggled with the issue of slavery, and the terrible Civil War began. Ships and gunboats of the Union and Confederacy fought to control the Mississippi. In the Battle of New Orleans, Union ships traveled upriver from the Gulf of Mexico to capture the city and master the river. After the Union won the war in 1865, river traffic helped deliver goods from Canada to the Gulf of Mexico and from the Atlantic Ocean to western territories.

14,000 BCE   500 CE   1200 CE   1682 CE   1780 CE   1811 CE   1825 CE

Groundwater packed with gravel, sand, silt, and clay lies under about 32,000 square miles of the Mississippi River valley. It feeds wells and irrigates crops along the river.

A human tide of land-hungry pioneers continued to pour across the river. By 1880, huge steam-powered paddleboats traveled up and down the Mississippi. Along with settlers, steamboats carried adventurers, musical revues, and gamblers.

To promote settlement farther west, the Army Corps of Engineers spent years improving traffic on the Mississippi. Known as "the Graveyard" by river men, it had hundreds of sunken wrecks trapped beneath its surface. The corps removed hidden trees, dredged sandbars, dynamited rock, and built canals to stabilize the dangerous waters of the Mississippi and its tributaries.

14,000 BCE   500 CE   1200 CE   1682 CE   1780 CE   1811 CE   1825 CE

*F*ish and wildlife abound along the Mississippi River. More than a hundred species of fish make it a major migration corridor for millions of raptors, waterfowl, and other birds. They fly south from frigid northern areas to the warmer Gulf of Mexico. Lakes, uplands, marshes, and wetlands provide breeding grounds for wintering birds, including the bald eagle.

Devastating floods continued to plague communities along the river. Settlers were unprepared for loss of crops, homes, and lives. To protect farms and towns on the floodplain, communities united to build 20-foot-high earthen levees from city to city for more than 1,600 miles, longer than the Great Wall of China!

Congress paid for the removal of underwater snags in the upper Mississippi River. Tens of thousands of submerged trees were removed by 1900.

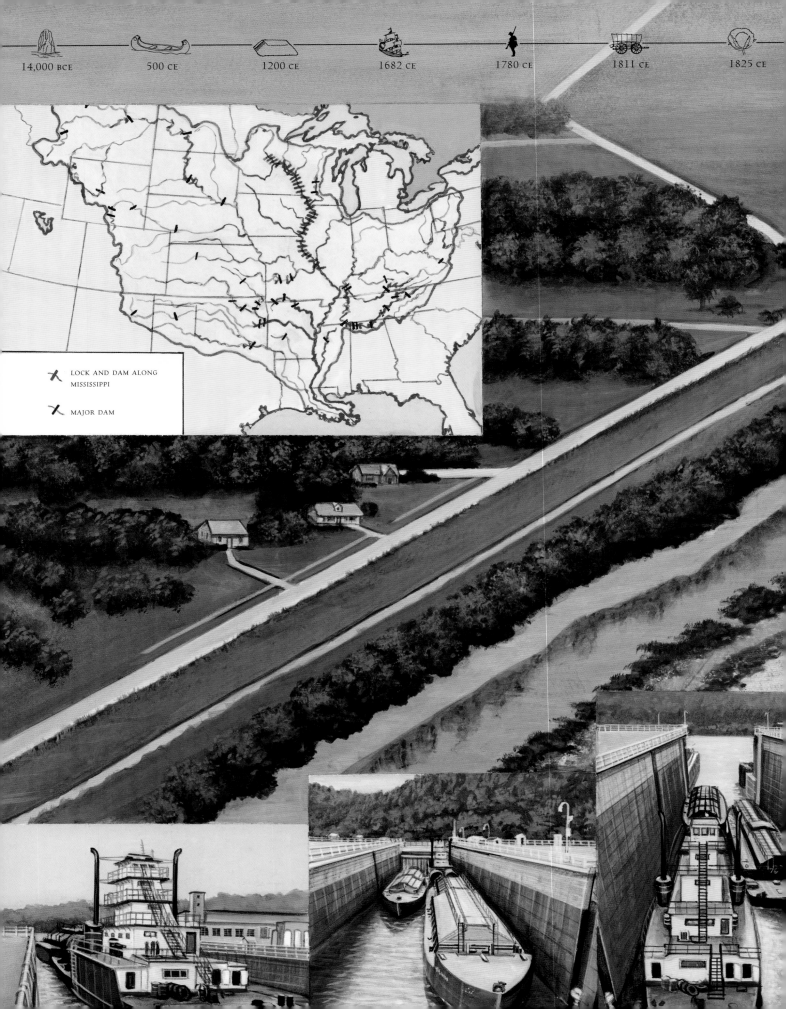

LOCK AND DAM ALONG
MISSISSIPPI

MAJOR DAM

Narrow forests separate flat prairies along the floodplain. Thickly wooded areas provide deep, widespread roots that cling to soil. These root systems protect the land from being washed away by devastating floods.

The Mississippi River flood of 1927, one of the worst in American history, caused more than two hundred deaths. Over eight hundred thousand people evacuated their homes. The corps was determined to deepen shallow areas and protect adjacent lands from overwhelming floods.

Beginning in 1930, they spent decades building twenty-nine locks and dams to manage the 420-foot difference in river elevation between Minneapolis-St. Paul, Minnesota, and St. Louis, Missouri. The system works like a staircase, using gravity to manipulate water levels and prevent flooding. This also keeps the river at least 9 feet deep for barges that carry freight and powerful tugboats that push them.

Nutrient-rich deposits are carried south by the relentless current to fertile lowlands of the Mississippi River Delta. Created over millions of years as the river laid down new routes to its mouth in the Gulf of Mexico, the Delta covers 12,000 square miles from Memphis, Tennessee, to New Orleans, Louisiana. Thousands more square miles of the Delta lie underwater.

Along the Gulf, Delta cities are pounded by destructive ocean-borne storms. Hurricane Camille, one of the worst ever to hit the United States, smashed the area in 1969 with winds greater than 200 miles per hour and tides over 20 feet high. The terrible storm washed away houses and buried farms across the Mississippi River valley from Louisiana to Florida. More than 250 people died, and thousands were left homeless.

14,000 BCE   500 CE   1200 CE   1682 CE   1780 CE   1811 CE   1825 CE

1846 CE

1862 CE

1880 CE

1900 CE

1930 CE

1969 CE

TODAY

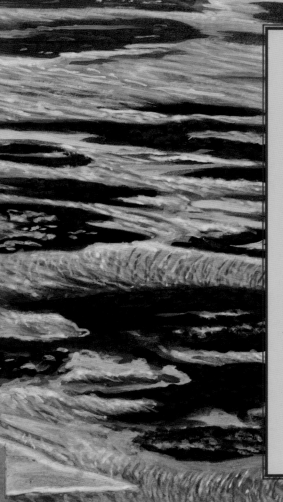

About 100 miles south of New Orleans, the tiny village of Pilottown balances on stiltlike pilings as river currents mix with ocean tides. This watery settlement stands at Head of Passes, the official end of the Mississippi River. Fifteen million gallons of river water and silt pour into the Gulf every second. One cubic mile of mud is added to its waters each year.

The river has endured all manner of natural disasters. It has seen devastating wars and has been redirected by modern engineering. As it has for millions of years, the Mississippi continues to flow like a twisted ribbon through thousands of miles of the American heartland, from a tiny northern freshwater stream to the vast reaches of a salty southern sea.